DRAW
50
CATS

Other books by Lee J. Ames:

DRAW, DRAW, DRAW
DRAW 50 ANIMALS
DRAW 50 BOATS, SHIPS, TRUCKS AND TRAINS
DRAW 50 DINOSAURS AND OTHER PREHISTORIC
        ANIMALS
DRAW 50 AIRPLANES, AIRCRAFT AND
        SPACECRAFT
DRAW 50 FAMOUS FACES
DRAW 50 FAMOUS CARTOONS
DRAW 50 VEHICLES
DRAW 50 BUILDINGS AND OTHER STRUCTURES
DRAW 50 DOGS
DRAW 50 FAMOUS STARS
DRAW 50 MONSTERS, CREEPS, SUPERHEROES,
        DEMONS, DRAGONS, NERDS, DIRTS,
        GHOULS, GIANTS, VAMPIRES, ZOMBIES,
        AND OTHER CURIOSA . . .
DRAW 50 HORSES
DRAW 50 ATHLETES
DRAW 50 CARS, TRUCKS, AND MOTORCYCLES
MAKE 25 CRAYON DRAWINGS OF THE CIRCUS
MAKE 25 FELT-TIP DRAWINGS OUT WEST
THE DOT, LINE AND SHAPE CONNECTION

DRAW 50 CATS

LEE J. AMES

Doubleday

NEW YORK   LONDON   TORONTO   SYDNEY   AUCKLAND

Published by Doubleday, a division of
Bantam Doubleday Dell Publishing Group, Inc.,
666 Fifth Avenue, New York, New York 10103.

Doubleday and the portrayal of an anchor with a
dolphin are trademarks of Doubleday, a division of
Bantam Doubleday Dell Publishing Group, Inc.

Printed in the United States of America

4   6   8   9   7   5

BG

Library of Congress Cataloging in Publication Data:

Ames, Lee J.
  Draw 50 cats.
  Summary: Step-by-step instructions on how to draw a variety of cats, including
domestic breeds, wild cats, cuddly kittens, and celebrity cats.
    1. Cats in art—Juvenile literature.   2. Drawing—Technique—Juvenile literature.
[1. Cats in art.   2. Drawing—Technique]   I. Title.   II. Title: Draw fifty cats.
NC780.A4818   1986   743′.6974428   86-8964
ISBN 0-385-23484-8
ISBN 0-385-23485-6 (lib. bdg.)

This is for my lovely new grandkitten,
Lauren Michelle . . .

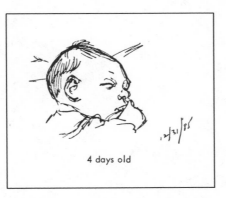

4 days old

Thanks, Warren, for all your help.

TO THE READER

This book will show you a way to draw a wide variety of your favorite felines. You need not start with the first illustration. Choose whichever you wish. When you have decided, follow the step-by-step method shown. *Very lightly* and *carefully,* sketch out step number one. However, this step, which is the easiest, should be done *most carefully.* Step number two is added right to step number one, also lightly and also very carefully. Step number three is sketched right on top of numbers one and two. Continue this way to the last step.

It may seem strange to ask you to be extra careful when you are drawing what seem to be the easiest first steps, but this is most important because a careless mistake at the beginning may spoil the whole picture at the end. As you sketch out each step, watch the spaces between the lines, as well as the lines, and see that they are the same. After each step, you may want to lighten your work by pressing it with a kneaded eraser (available at art supply stores).

When you have finished, you may want to redo the final step in India ink with a fine brush or pen. When the ink is dry, use the kneaded eraser to clean off the pencil lines. The eraser will not affect the India ink.

Here are some suggestions: In the first few steps, even when all seems quite correct, you might do well to hold your work up to a mirror. Sometimes the mirror shows that you've twisted the drawing off to one side without being aware of it. At first you may find it difficult to draw the boxes, triangles, or circles, or just to make the pencil go where you wish. Don't be discouraged. The more you practice, the more control you will develop. Use a compass or a ruler if you wish; professional artists do! The only equipment you'll need will be a medium or soft pencil, paper, the kneaded eraser and, if you wish, a compass, ruler, pen or brush.

The first steps in this book are shown darker than necessary so that they can be clearly seen. (Keep your own work very light.)

Remember, there are many other ways and methods to make drawings. This book shows just one method. Why don't you seek out other ways and methods to make drawings—from teachers, from libraries and, most important . . . from inside yourself?

LEE J. AMES

TO THE PARENT OR TEACHER

"Leslie can draw a Siamese cat better than anybody else!" Such peer acclaim and encouragement generate incentive. Contemporary methods of art instruction (freedom of expression, experimentation, self-evaluation of competence and growth) provide a vigorous, fresh-air approach for which we must all be grateful.

New ideas need not, however, totally exclude the old. One such is the "follow me, step-by-step" approach. In my young learning days this method was so common, and frequently so exclusive, that the student became nothing more than a pantographic extension of the teacher. In those days it was excessively overworked.

This does not mean that the young hand is never to be guided. Rather, specific guiding is fundamental. Step-by-step guiding that produces satisfactory results is valuable even when the means of accomplishment are not fully understood by the student.

The novice with a musical instrument is frequently taught to play simple melodies as quickly as possible, well before he learns the most elemental scratchings at the surface of music theory. The resultant self-satisfaction, pride in accomplishment, can be a significant means of providing motivation. And all from mimicking an instructor's "Do-as-I-do . . ."

Mimicry is prerequisite for developing creativity. We learn the use of our tools by mimicry. Then we can use those tools for creativity. To this end I would offer the budding artist the opportunity to memorize or mimic (rote-like, if you wish) the making of "pictures." "Pictures" he has been anxious to be able to draw.

The use of this book should be available to anyone who *wants* to try another way of flapping his wings. Perhaps he or she will then get off the ground when a friend says, "Leslie can draw a Siamese cat better than anybody else!"

LEE J. AMES

DRAW
50
CATS

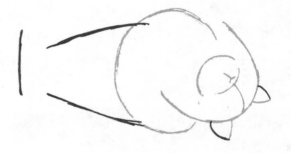

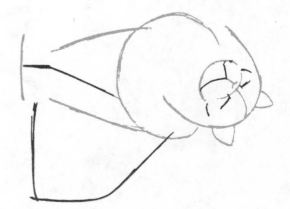

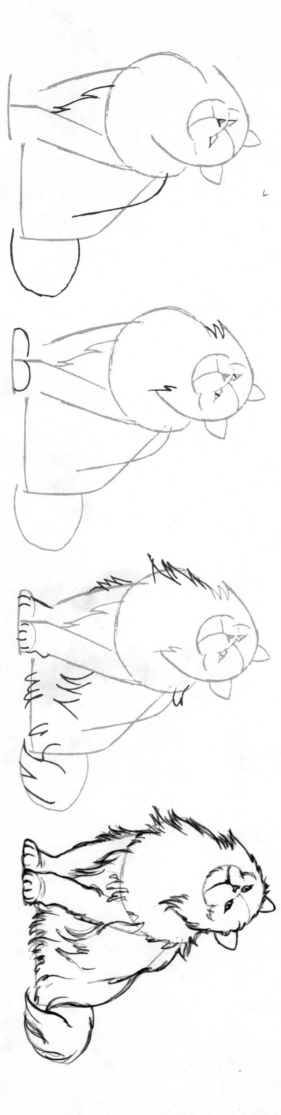

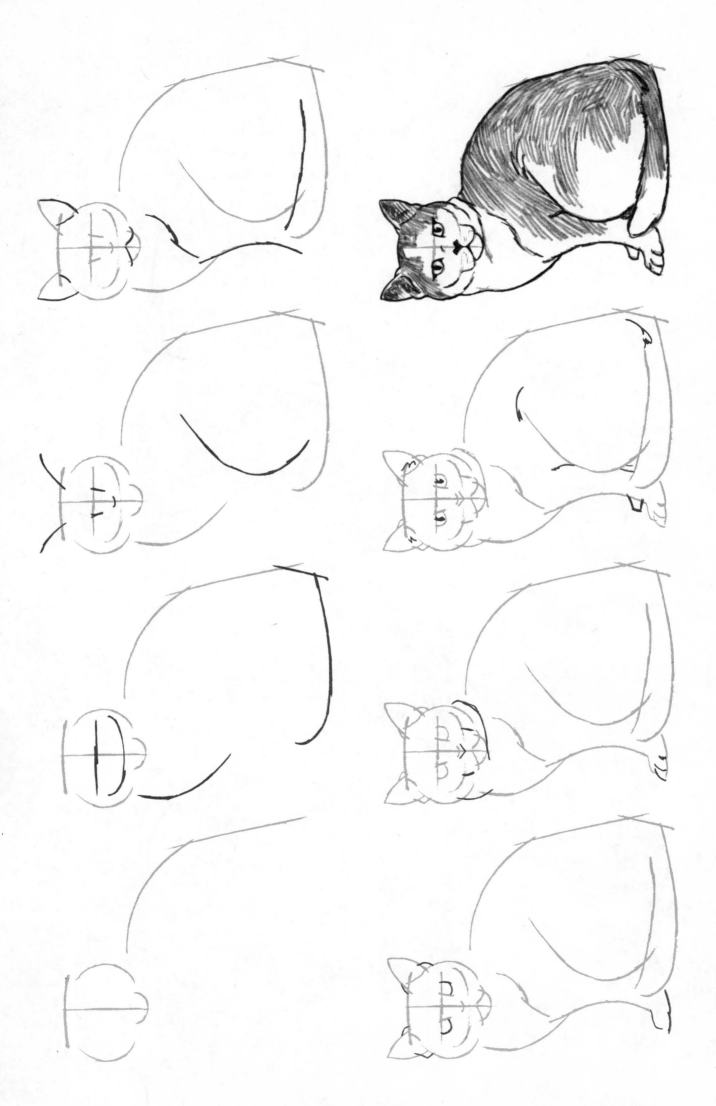

American Shorthair

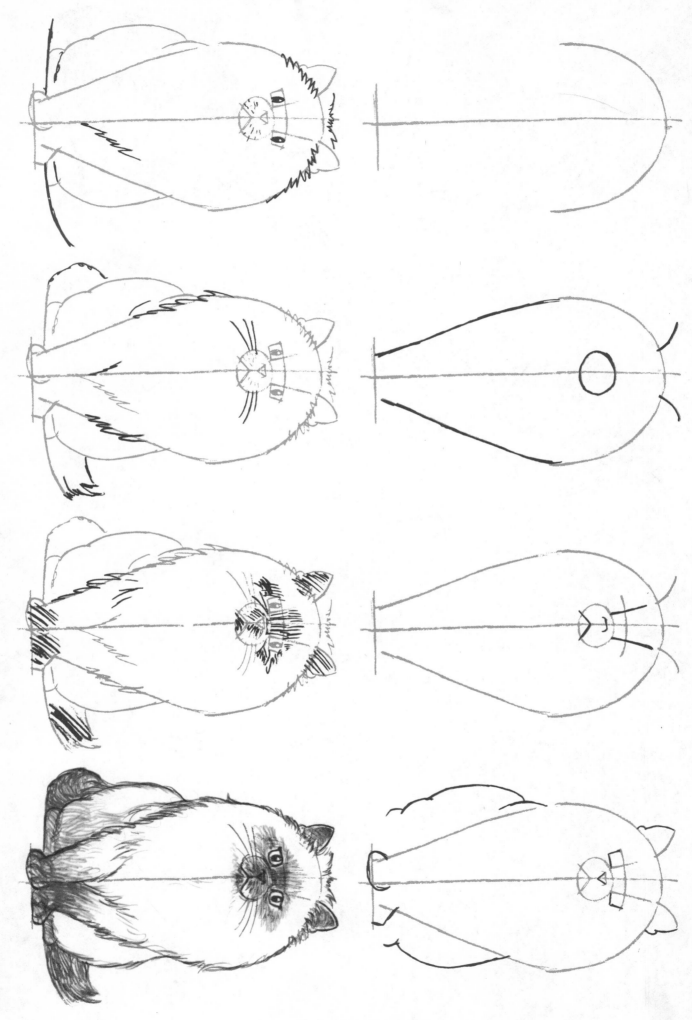

Himalayan Blue Point

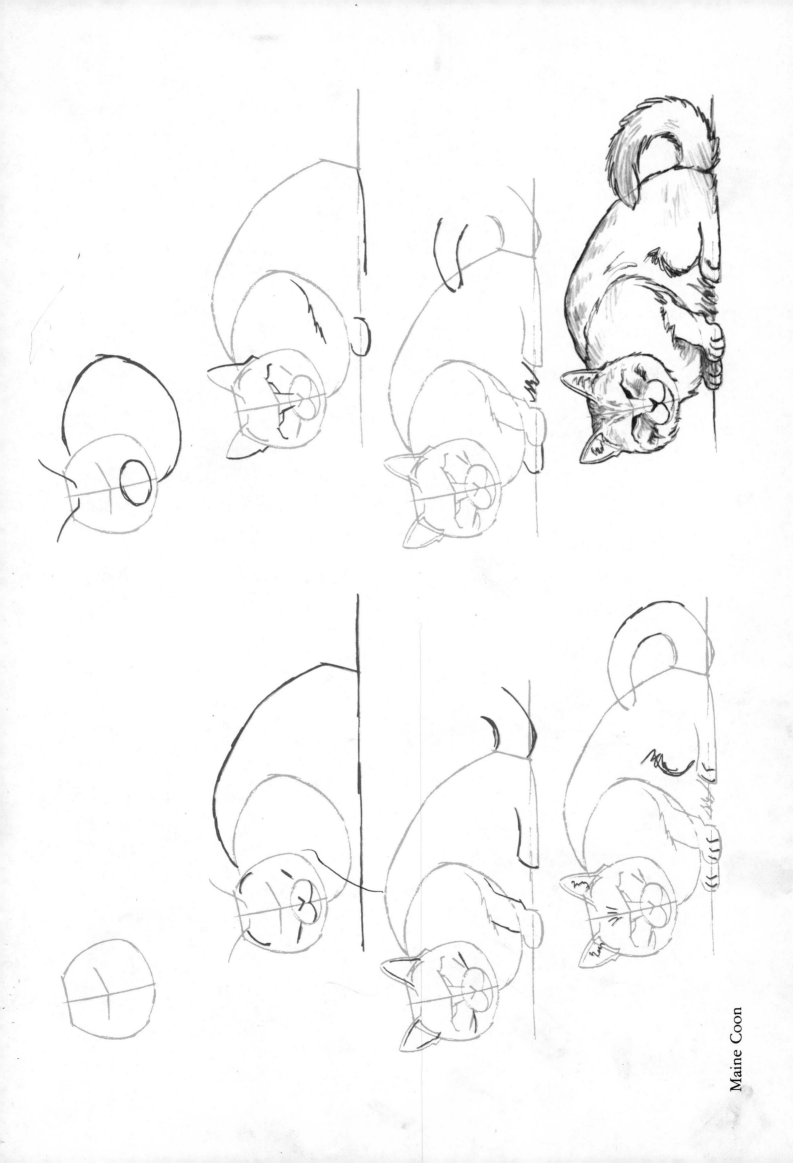

Maine Coon

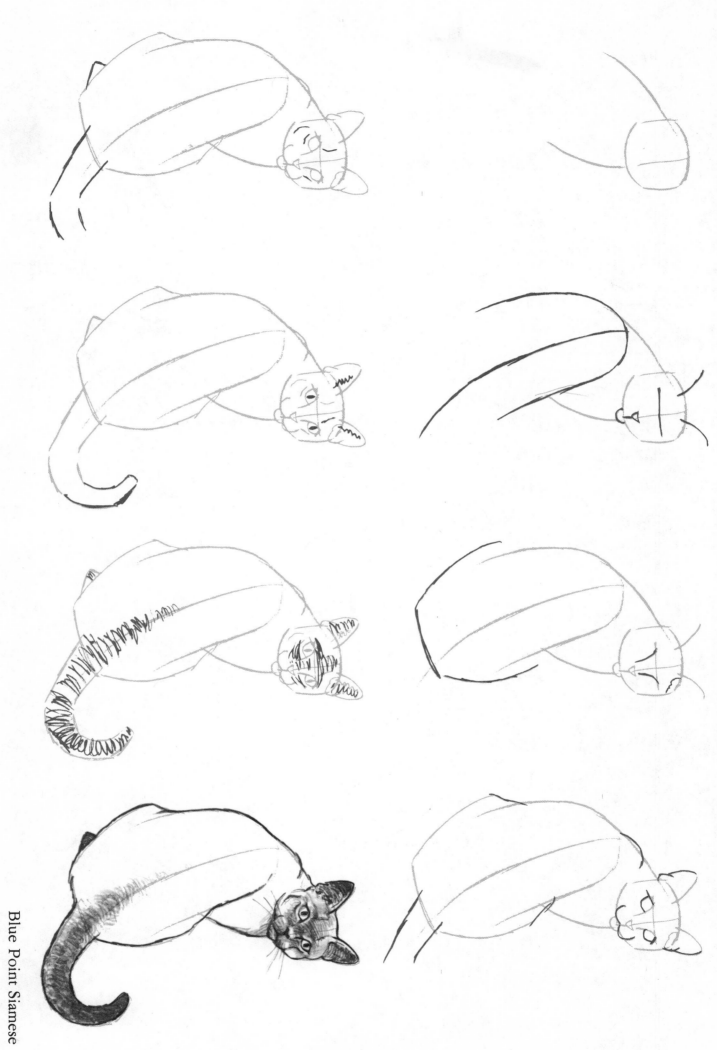

Blue Point Siamese

Persian

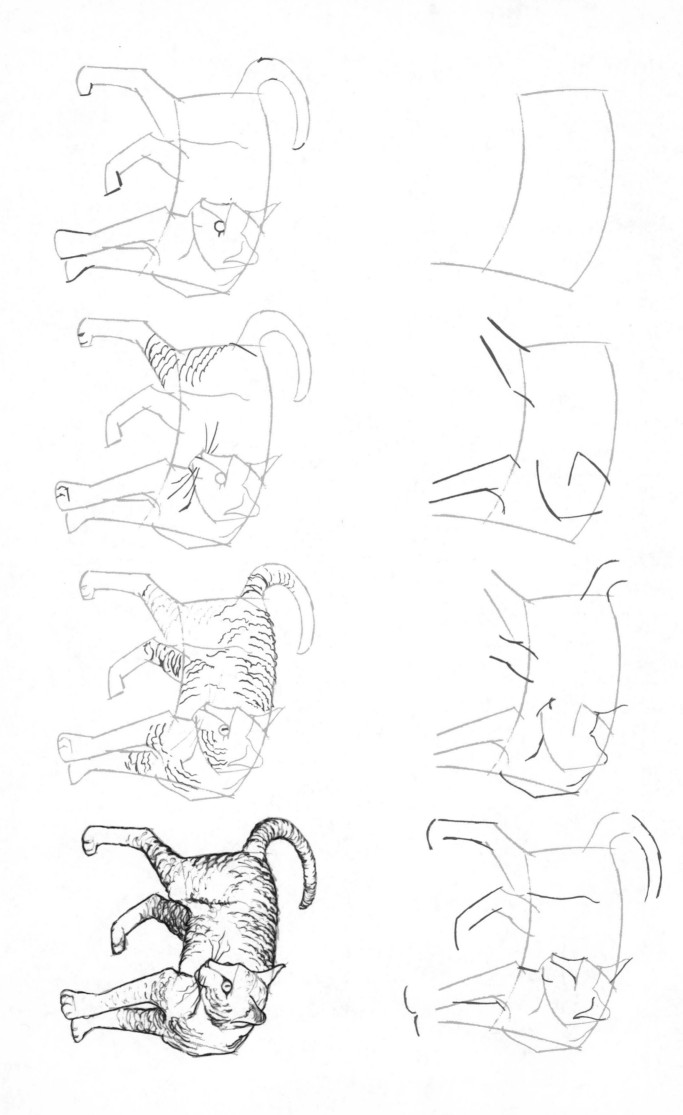

Rex

Manx

Egyptian Mau

Long-haired Tabby

Birman

Havana Brown

Abyssinian

Burmese

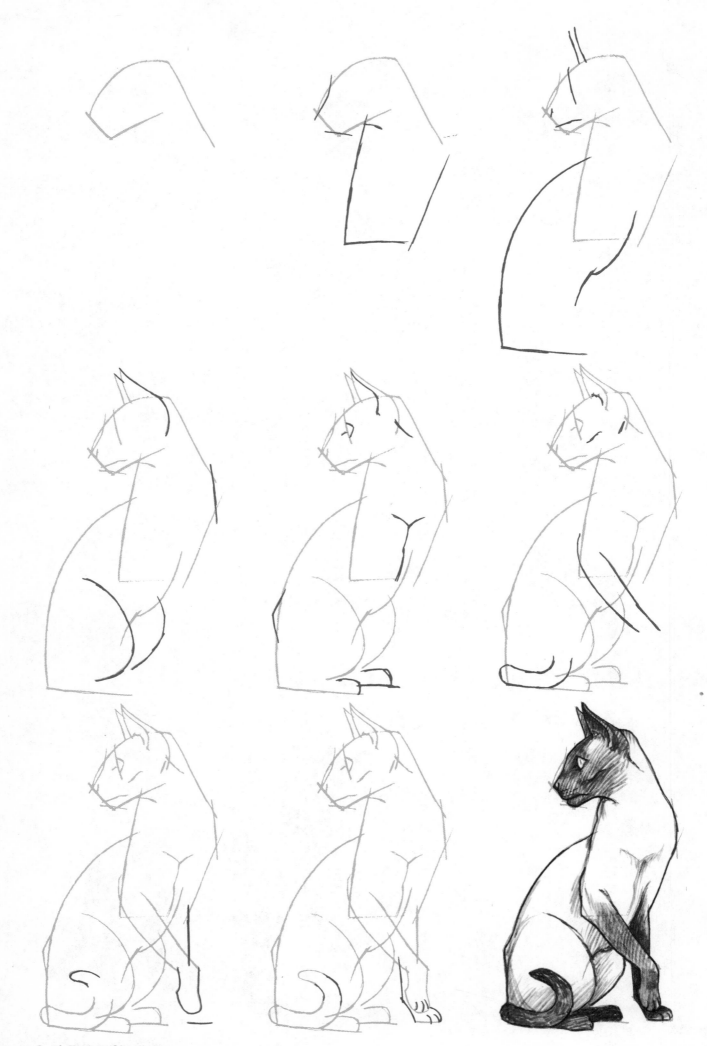

Seal Point Siamese

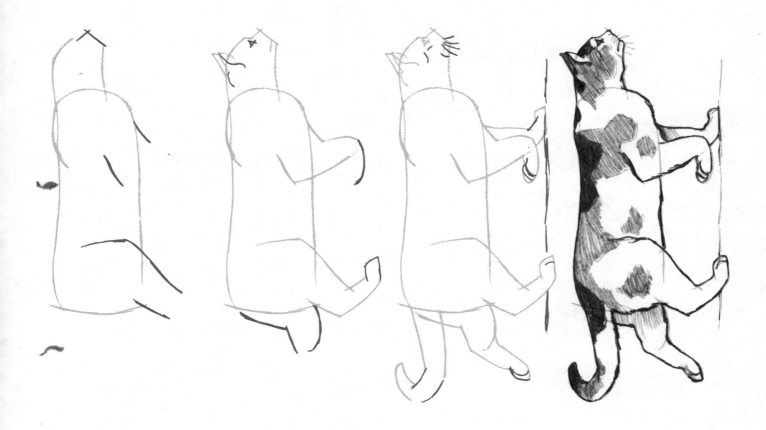

Calico

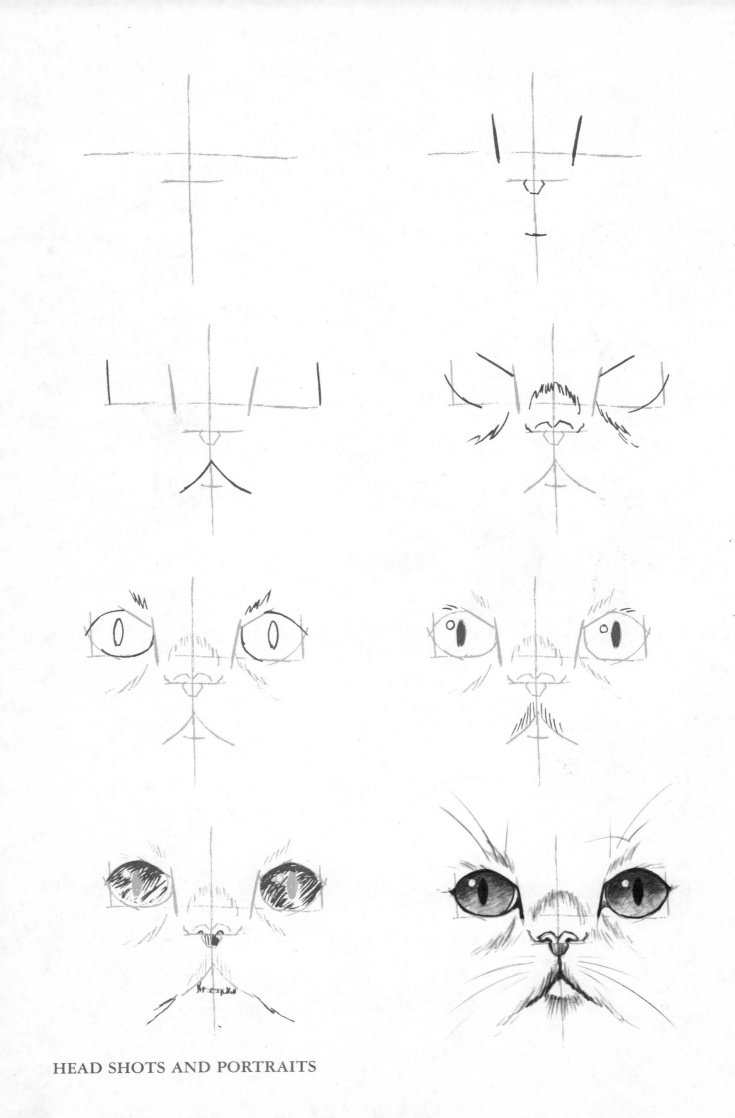

HEAD SHOTS AND PORTRAITS

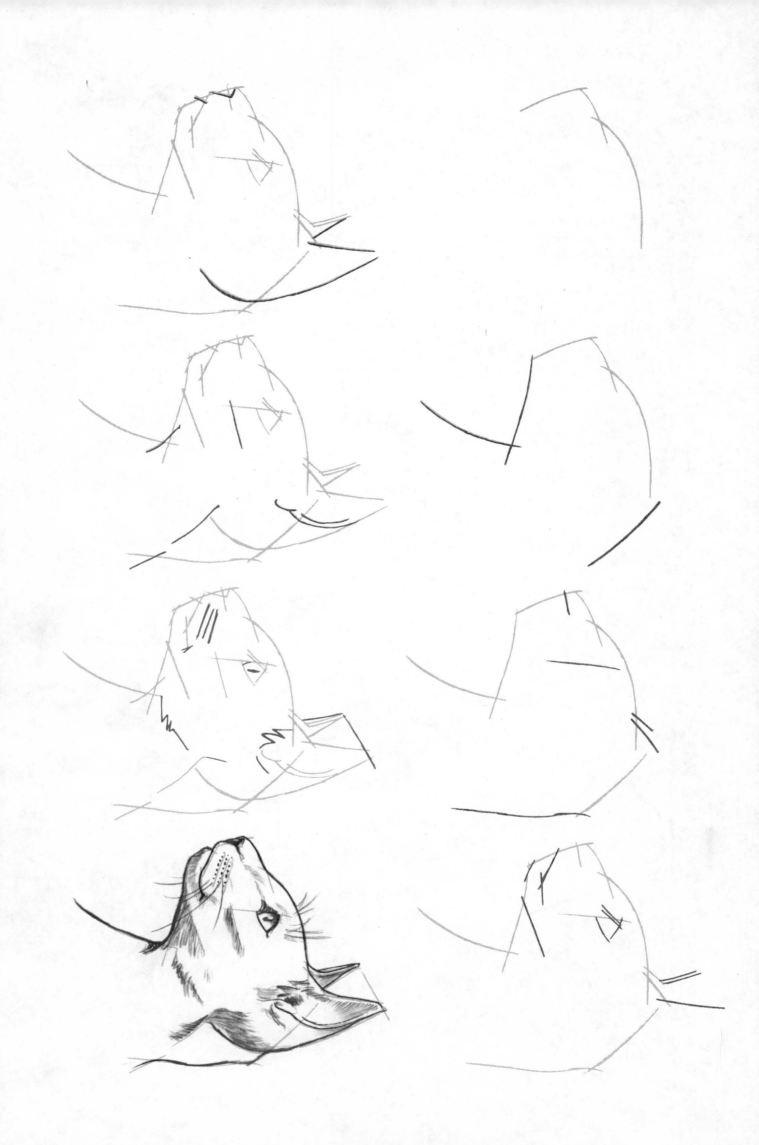

WILD CATS
Jaguar

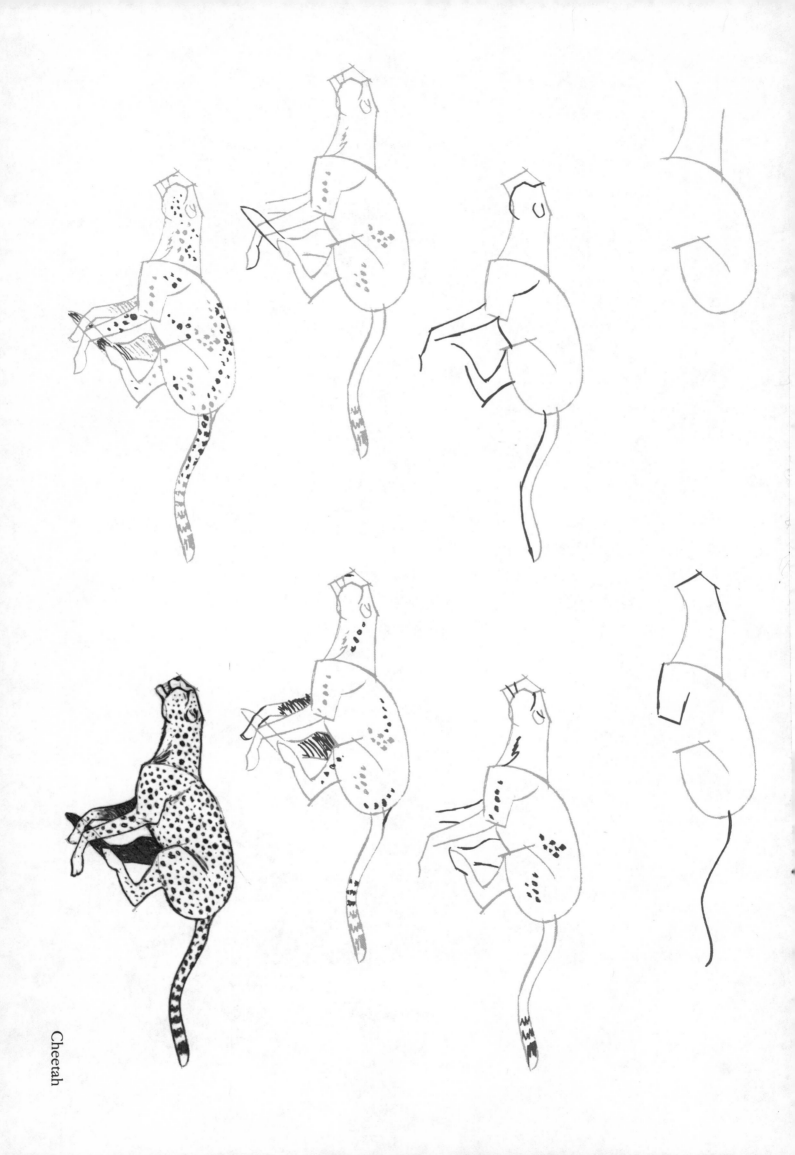

Cheetah

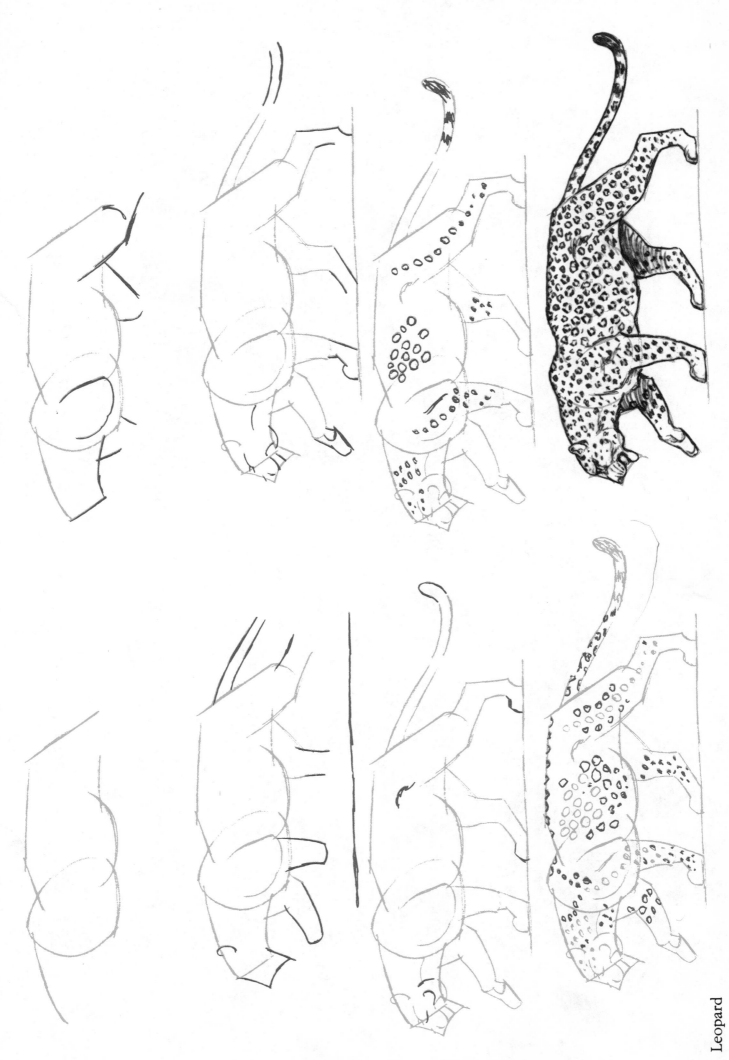

Leopard

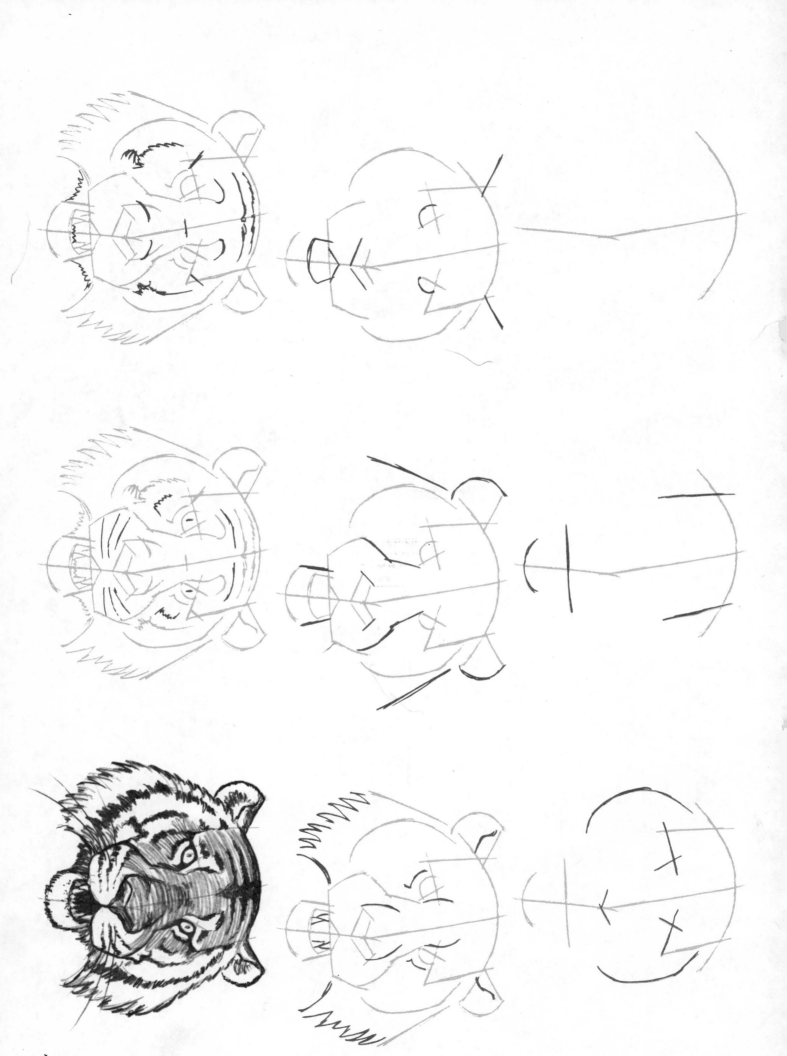

Tiger

Bobcat

Caracal

Cougar

Lion

FAMOUS CATS
Morris, the 9 Lives® Cat
© 1986 Star-Kist Foods, Inc., owner of the registered trademark,
Morris, the 9 Lives® Cat. Used with permission.

Top Cat
© 1986 Hanna-Barbera Productions, Inc.

Baby Puss
© 1986 Hanna-Barbera Productions, Inc.

Snagglepuss
© 1986 Hanna-Barbera Productions, Inc.

Felix the Cat
© 1986 Felix the Cat Productions, Inc.
FELIX THE CAT reprinted with special permission of King Features Syndicate, Inc.

KITTENS
Kitten takes its first steps.

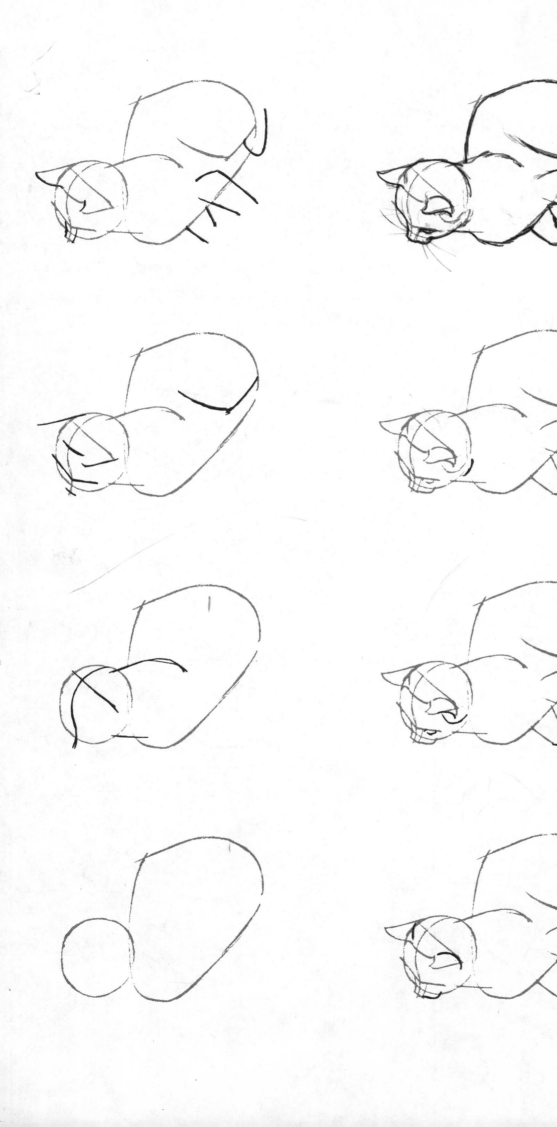

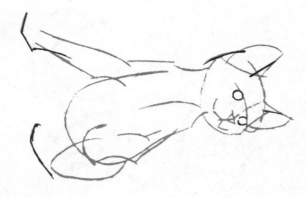
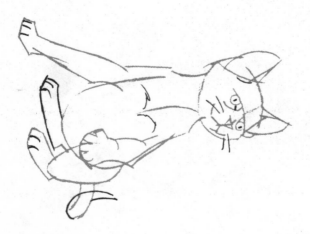
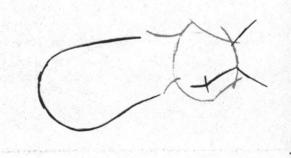
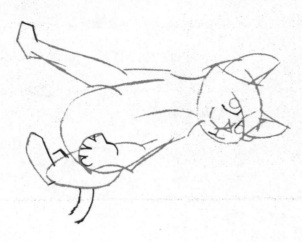
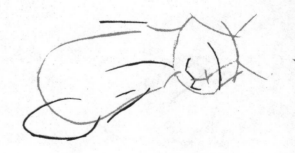
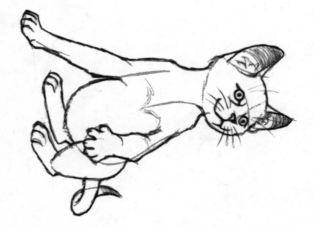

Siamese kitten

Persian kitten

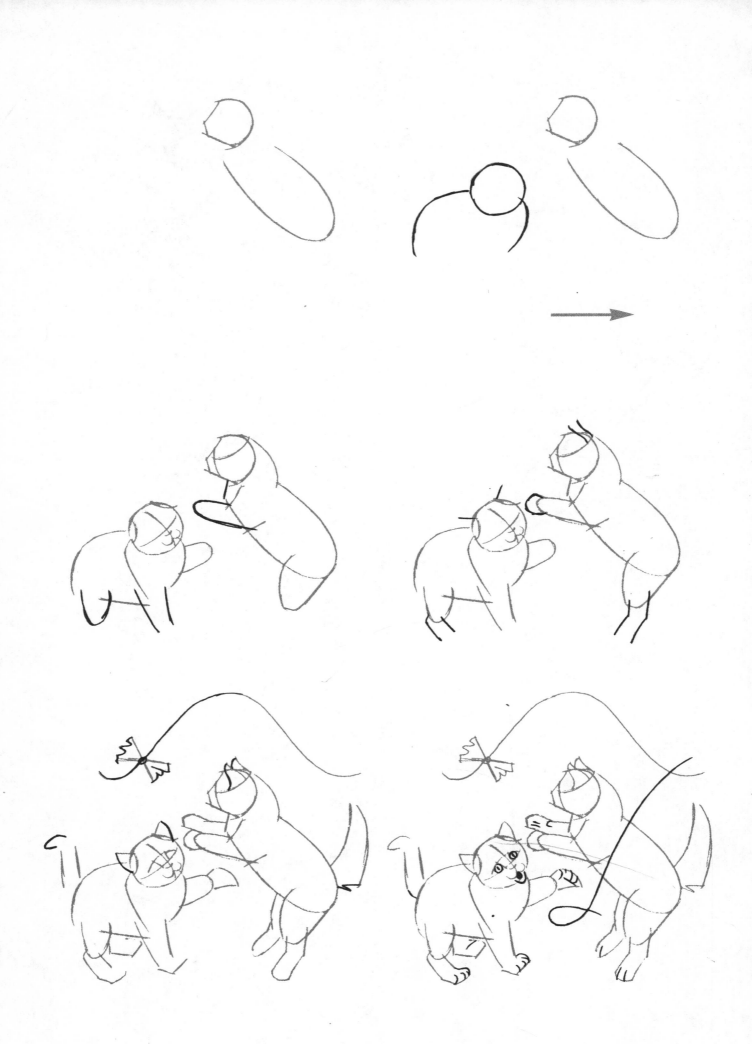

Kittens at play

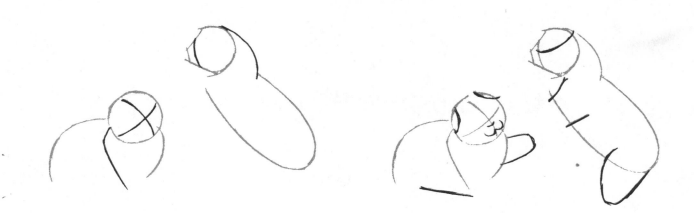

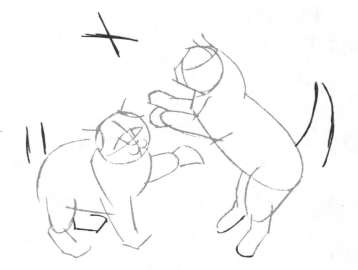

COMMON BEHAVIOR
Offensive posture

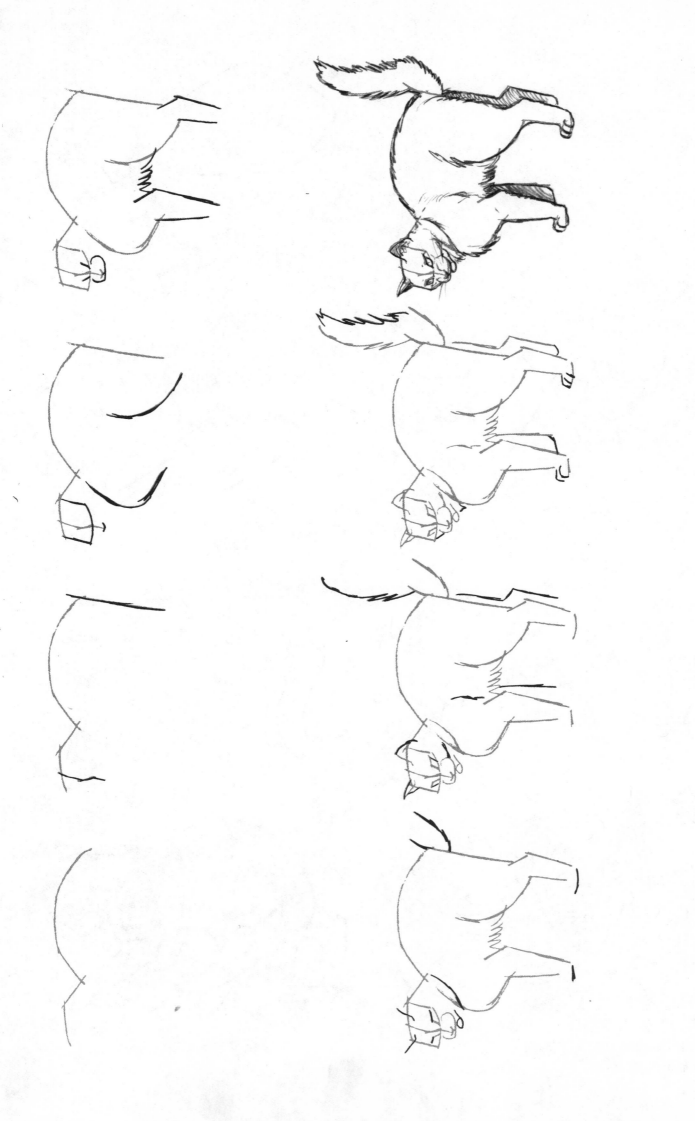

Defensive posture

At play

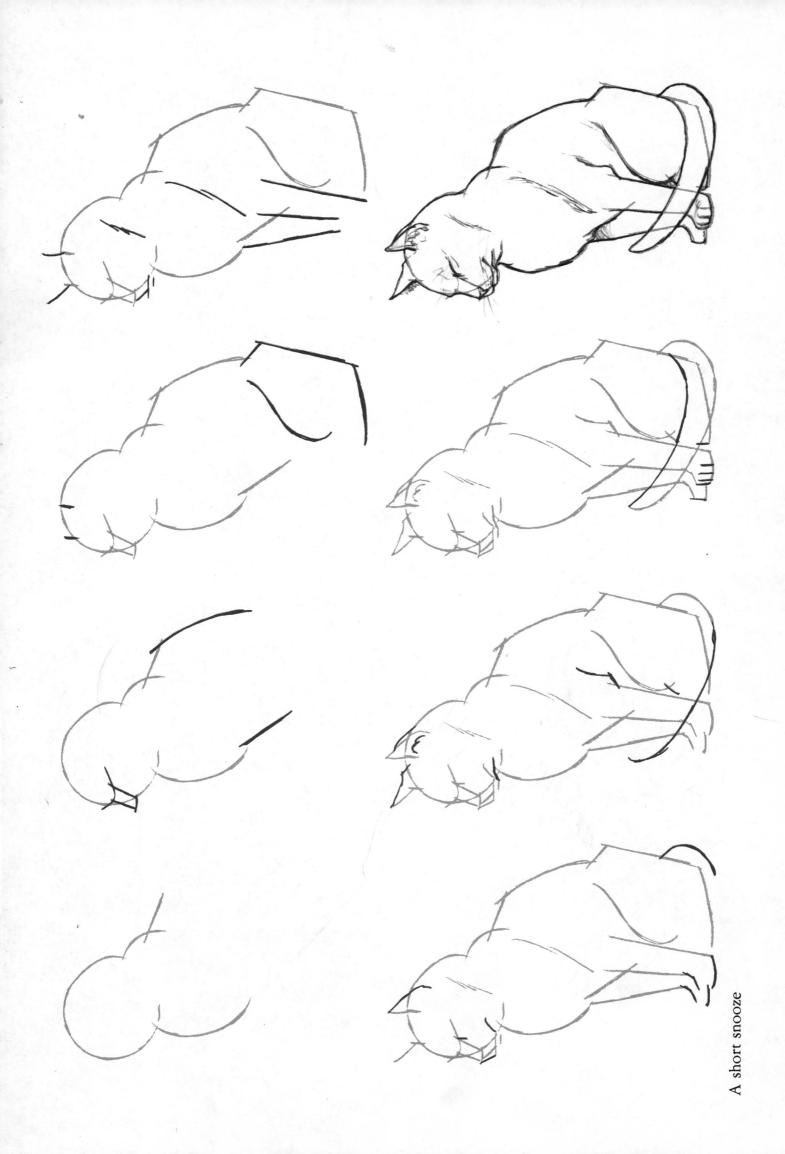

A short snooze

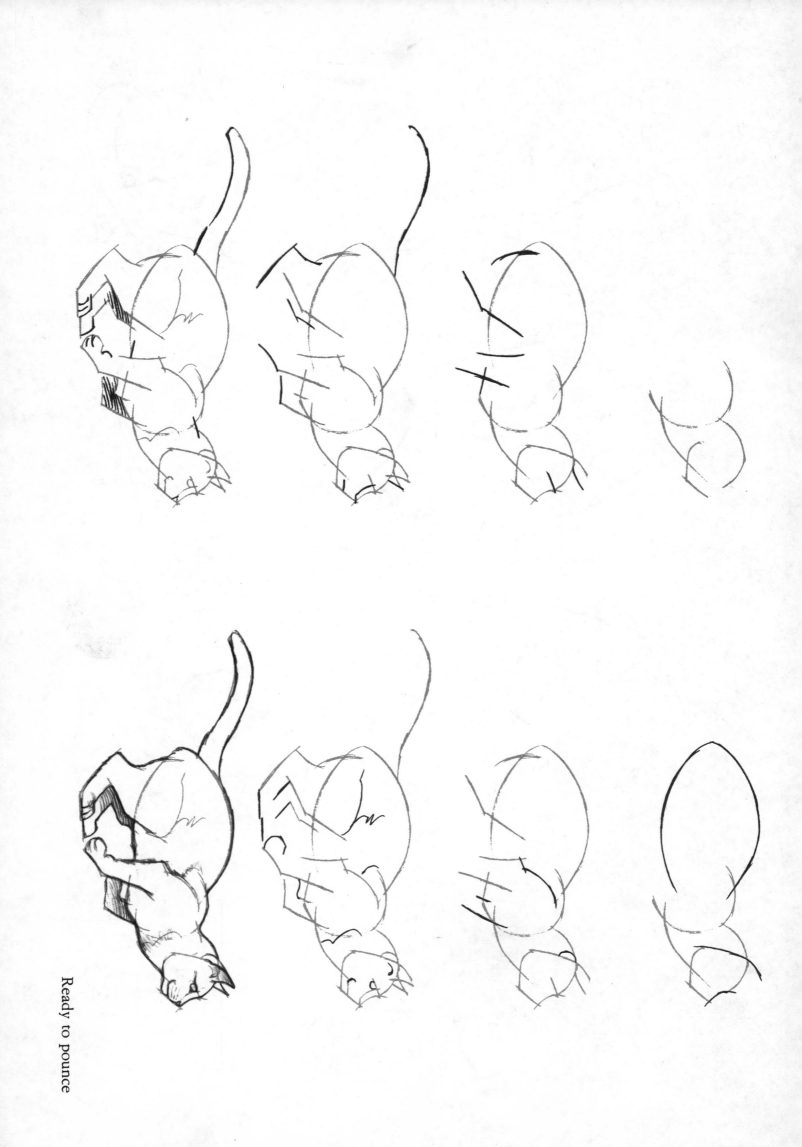

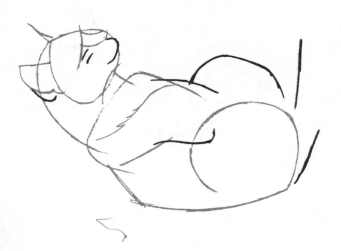

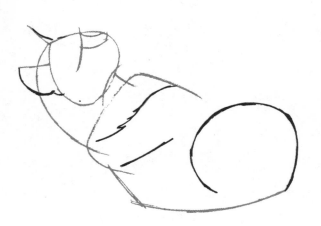

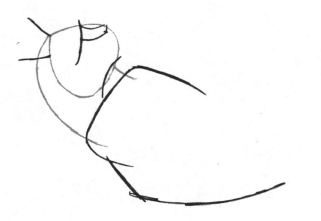

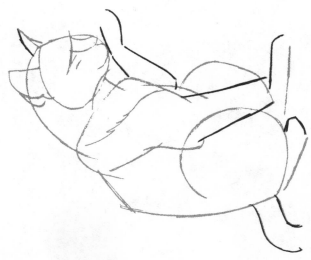

Grooming

A curious Tabby

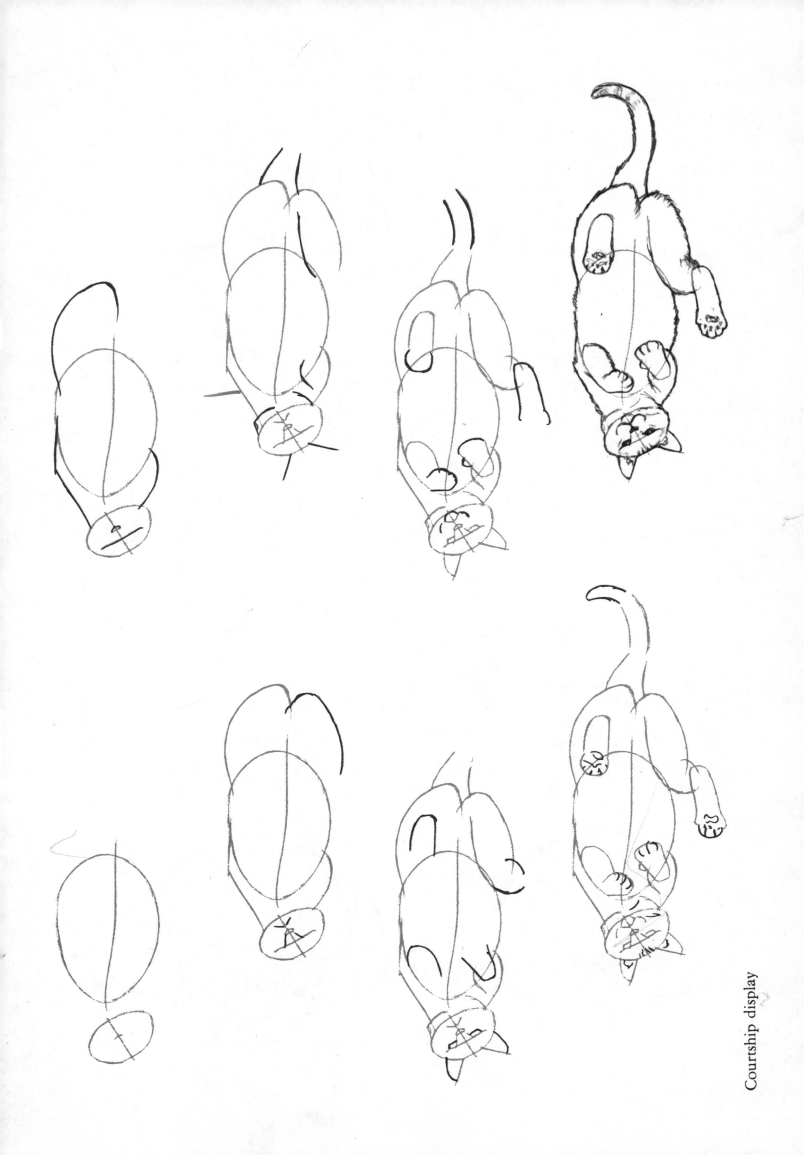

Courtship display

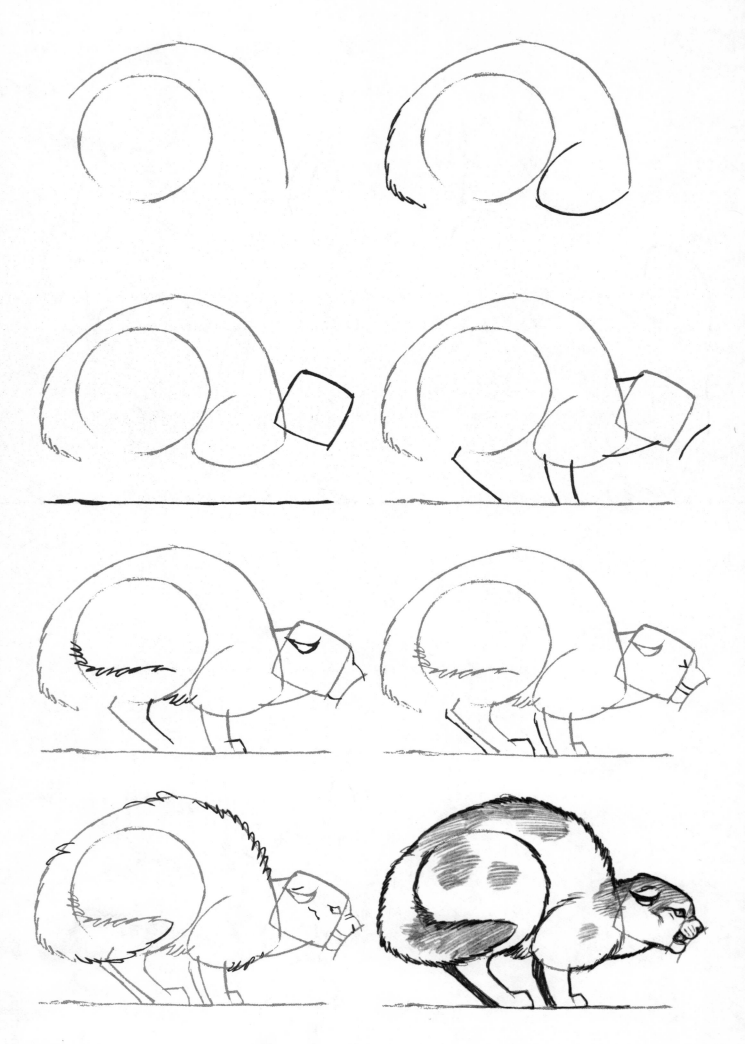

Frightened

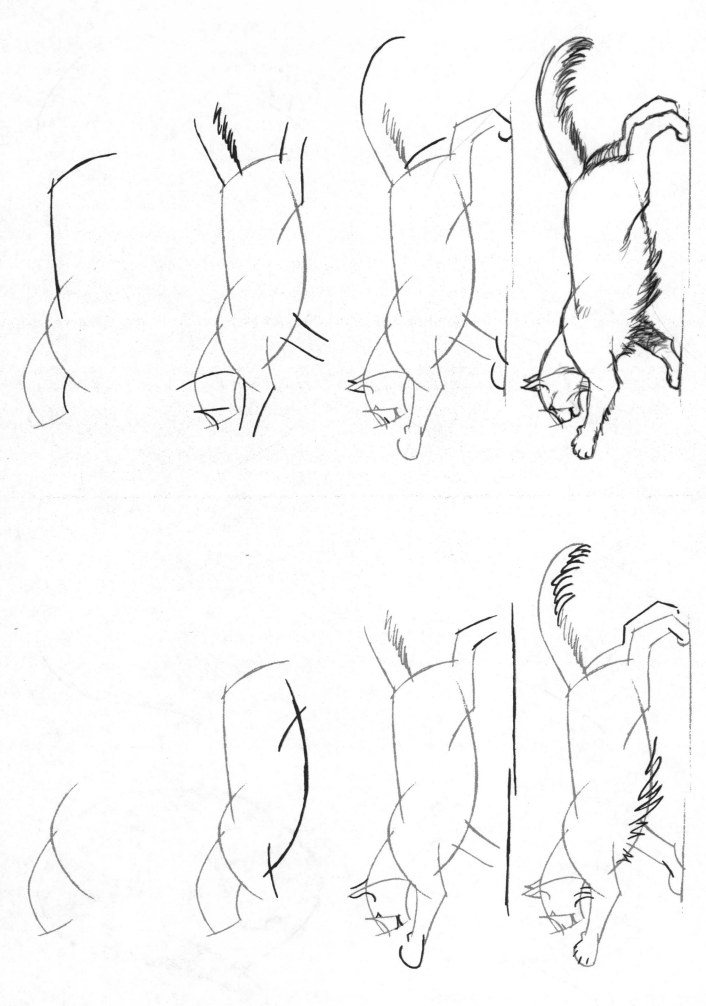

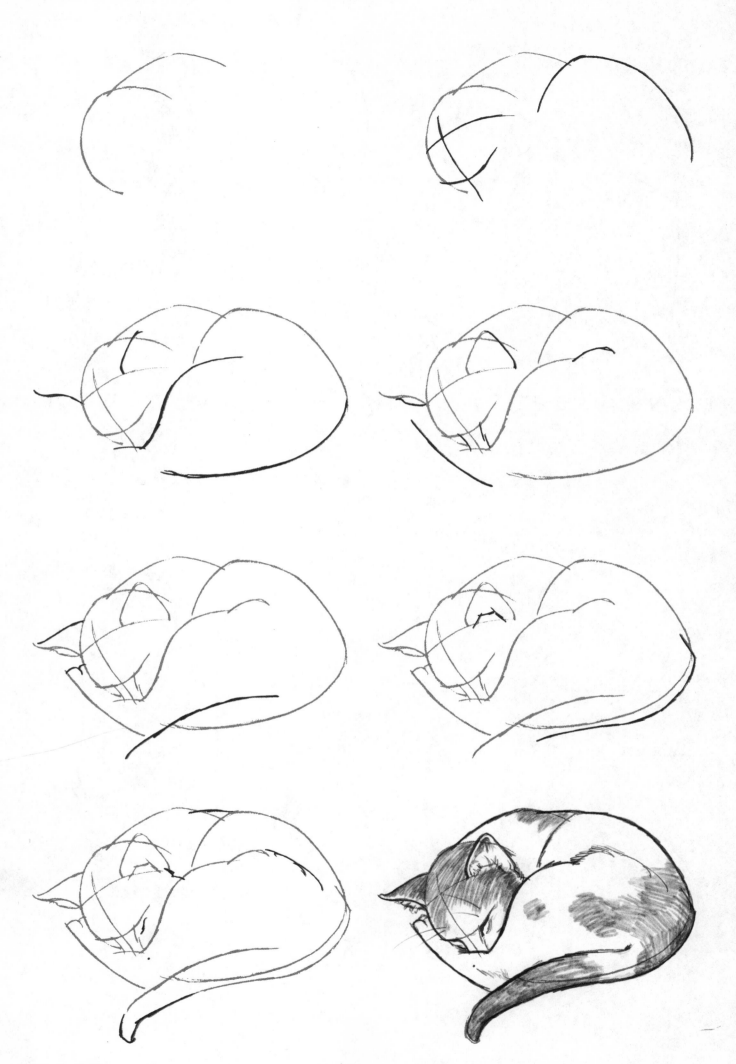

Good night